A Place for Wonder

The Story of the Giant Forest
of Sequoia National Park

Reflections at Crescent Meadow

By William C. Tweed
Published by the Sequoia Natural History Association

First Edition
First Printing May 2002

Printed in the United States
ISBN 1-878441-15-9

Written by William C. Tweed
Edited by Marilyn Norton
Project coordination and layout by Mark Tilchen
Typesetting and text design by Carl and Irving Printers

Published by
Sequoia Natural History Association
HCR 89, Box 10
Three Rivers, CA 93271
559-565-3759
www.sequoiahistory.org

The non-profit Sequoia Natural History Association works in partnership with the National Park Service to provide educational publications and programs for Sequoia and Kings Canyon National Parks and Devils Postpile National Monument. All income of the Association is devoted to national park scientific and educational endeavors.

Photo Credits
Tom Gamache For Wandering Around Outdoors: Front cover
Steve Bumgardner: Pages 15, 16, 18
Dick Burns: Title page, pages 1, 2 top right, 3 bottom, 4, 8, 9
Heidi Crouch: Back cover
Mark Tilchen: Pages 2 top left, 5
National Park Service collection: Pages 2 bottom, 3 top, 6, 10, 12, 13

A Place for Wonder

The mountaintop plateau stands boldly like the foredeck of some ancient, proud ship, a small triangle of gentle terrain in a land of enormous and some-times violent physical relief. On this small plateau grows an amazing forest — the largest trees on earth. Since the late nineteenth century, it has been known as the Giant Forest. It is the crowning glory of Sequoia National Park.

The Sierra Nevada, the four-hundred-mile-long mountain range that defines the eastern flank of California, contains by traditional count about seventy-five sequoia groves, an archipelago of forest islands that constitutes the entire natural range of the world's largest trees. Of these the Giant Forest was identified as long ago as 1875 and described by no less eminent an expert than naturalist John Muir, as the "finest."

Imagine a well watered, gently rolling mountain-top covered with a forest of immense proportions. Pines and fir trees commonly grow to be 3-5 feet (.9 - 1.5 meters) in basal diameter and more than 150 feet (46 meters) tall, yet even these huge trees are dwarfed by the giant sequoias that inhabit this mile-high realm. In the Giant Forest grow thousands of trees greater than ten feet (3 meters) in diameter, and the largest exceed thirty feet (9 meters) at the base. These giants often grow in dense stands near lush, green, forest-bounded wetlands. But just below the rim of the plateau, conditions are startlingly different. Almost immediately, steep, dry slopes of often-impenetrable brush replace the huge trees and verdant meadows. Above the grove, to the east, the change is just as startling. The sequoias disappear, replaced by smaller, more cold tolerant forest species. Within a few miles, as altitude is gained, all trees quit, and the mountains rise in barren grandeur. Alta Peak, the 11,200 foot (3413 meters) mountain that overlooks the grove, has snow most years — even on its sunny southwestern side — from October into June.

On this unique plateau, giant sequoias apparently discover exactly what they seek, for here they grow

Visitors explore Giant Forest's Round Meadow

more vigorously than anywhere else in their native range. Of the five largest trees in the world (all giant sequoias), four are in the Giant Forest, including the ultimate specimen — the General Sherman Tree. Of the sequoias larger than twenty feet (6 meters) in diameter, there are twice as many in Giant Forest as in any other grove.

Since it first attracted the attention of Euro-American pioneers in the mid-nineteenth century, this small, isolated tract of mountain land has inspired an amazing variety of human reactions. In a mere 150 years, it became a cattle ranch, the site of a Utopian colony, a military reservation of a sort, and ultimately an international tourist destination. John Muir wrote about it. The early National Park Service developed it as a destination resort and then came later to rethink its understanding of what the grove could sustain. The modern science of fire ecology grew in significant part out of the experience of managing the grove in the twentieth century. Today the grove continues to be the site of both large-scale restoration efforts as well as intense scientific monitoring. At the same time, nearly a million visitors wander its byways each year in awe.

Clearly the Giant Forest is a place rich in stories. On the following pages we will tell some of them.

Top left — Sun shines through giant sequoias on the edge of Round Meadow.

Top right — The Four Guardsman mark the entrance to Giant Forest on the Generals Highway

Bottom — Tunnel Log, on the road to Crescent Meadow, was created from a 1937 fallen sequoia

Place for Life

The Physical Setting

How does a small, gentle plateau come to be perched on a ridge top between two huge mountain canyons? After a century of geologic study, there is still no definitive answer. What is clear is that the granite country of the central and southern Sierra tends to erode over time into a terraced landscape of gentle plateaus separated by deep river canyons. As a plateau, the Giant Forest is far from unique. Other similar areas can be found to the north and south, but none shares its exact attributes. Two factors are critical to the Giant Forest as a sequoia grove. First, its altitude is between 6,400 and 7,200 feet (1950 meters and 2194 meters) and second, that the plateau is especially well-protected by topography from exposure to frigid down-slope winter air flows from higher altitudes.

On the ground, the plateau and the grove are not exactly synonymous. Along the southern rim, where the summer sun beats down with intensity, the sequoias do not drop below the canyon rim, and the forest comes to an abrupt end. On the northern side of the plateau, however, where the terrain is more sheltered from the intense summer sun and the climate thus damper, the trees slip down several drainages towards the Marble Fork of the Kaweah River. The plateau itself is not entirely level but rather is divided by a low ridge that separates the basins of Crescent and Log Meadows on the south from Round Meadow and Circle Meadow to the north. Small streams flow out of these meadows year round, suggesting just how generous a soil moisture regime the setting provides.

Adding character to the Giant Forest and its setting is another common Sierran geological process — dome formation. When it is not otherwise fractured by major cracks or other structural weaknesses, granite has the habit of weathering into rounded dome-like features. This process is intensified by the rock's habit of developing onion-like layers parallel to the surface, a process known as exfoliation. Exfoliation sites are common in the Giant Forest, as they

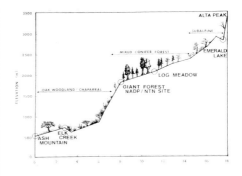

The Giant Forest is an ideal setting for the growth of giant sequoias.

Round Meadow, Giant Forest

are throughout the granite country of the entire Sierra Nevada. The plateau rim, where erosion has exposed the rock, is a particularly good place to look for such features. In the northwestern part of the grove, short trails lead to Beetle and Sunset rocks, both excellent examples of granitic exfoliation. Far more spectacular is Moro Rock, located along the grove's southern perimeter. By far the largest dome in the region, Moro Rock rises nearly 1500 feet (457 meters) above its southern base as a huge granite monolith. Steps lead to the top and in the process offer the best view most visitors obtain of the Giant Forest Plateau and its canyon-rimmed setting.

Climate and Life

The Giant Forest's mountain top location determines significant parts of the grove's climate. The regional climate is Mediterranean in nature with hot, dry summers, and cool, sometimes wet winters. At best, the winter storms are unreliable from year to year, with both very wet and very dry winters coming several times a decade. In this regional setting, the Sierra Nevada creates a distinctive localized climate. First, because the Sierra rises so far above the surrounding lowlands, its heights are significantly cooler, usually at least 15-20° F less than the neighboring lowlands. Then, since the winter storms come from the west, they collide with the mountains as they move inland with a resultant increase in precipitation that is striking. Because of the effect of the mountains, the middle altitudes of the Sierra receive an average of about five times as much precipitation as the San Joaquin Valley floor. Above 5,000 to 6,000 feet (1524 - 1828 meters), a majority of this precipitation falls as winter snow and although the amount of snow varies widely from year to year, extreme snowfalls can occur. In February 1933, one storm brought sixty inches (152 centimeters) of snow to Giant Forest in twenty-four hours!

The view from Moro Rock

This relatively wet and snowy mountain climate obviously creates a vegetation far different from the vegetation that has evolved to survive in lowland California. The result is the Sierra's famous mixed-conifer forest. Between about 5,000 and 9,000 feet (1524 - 2743 meters), the western slope of the southern Sierra is naturally clothed in a thick forest composed of more than a dozen species of conifer trees including numerous pines, two species of firs, and one species each of juniper and incense cedar. With their tall, narrow profiles and water-conserving needle-like leaves, all these conifers are well adapted to the southern Sierra's alternating waves of intense winter snows and nearly rainless summers. Within this extensive forest, where localized conditions are just right, giant sequoias also grow. We call these special places, which range in size from a few acres to several square miles, "sequoia groves." In this sense, the Giant Forest as a whole is a large sequoia grove comprising about 1,880 acres (761 hectares) of actual sequoia habitat within a somewhat larger perimeter.

Meadow and Forest

Within the Giant Forest, two habitats — meadow and forest — predominate, and each responds to its own set of natural rules.

The meadows, in summer lush, green, wildflower-filled swales, are wetlands — places too wet for trees to grow. These areas have developed over time in a number of places along watercourses on the plateau's surface where slopes are minimal and water drains away only very slowly. Some date back to before the end of the Ice Age 12,000 years ago, and since they tend to collect and preserve organic plant material, several have been cored with the hope of learning more about the environmental history of the surrounding forest. The fate of meadows depends entirely on their remaining too wet to be invaded by trees. All it takes to turn a meadow into a forest is a drop in the water table of as little as a foot or two.

The forest marches to the beat of an entirely different drummer. At first glance, filled as it is with

The scene in Giant Forest changes dramatically as winter snows transform the forest into a cross country skier's paradise

individual trees that live for hundreds of years, the forest seems enduring, unchanging. But actually, the forest is far more dynamic over time than the typical meadow. Key to this dynamism is the understanding that the nature and structure of the Sierran mixed-conifer forest is driven almost entirely by periodic cycles of disturbance, mostly in the form of fire.

Summer and autumn fires, ignited by occasional summer thunderstorms and sometimes in times past by Native Americans, once burned frequently in the Giant Forest. Tree ring studies document a fire frequency of five to fifteen years in most parts of the grove during at least the past several thousand years. When fires burned that frequently, their effect was profound. Frequent fires recycled fallen logs and branches, suppressed brush, and kept the forest relatively clean and open. Sun loving trees like pines and incense cedars, which require bright sunshine when they are seedlings, dominated much of the forest. Sequoias, as we will see on the next page, also enjoyed the benefits of fire.

A Home for Sequoias

Sequoias are picky trees when it comes to choosing where they will live — sprouting and enduring over time only when conditions exactly suit their needs. The need for soil moisture is clear. Sequoias grow best in areas with relatively abundant year-round water. Most of the forest habitat within the Sierra's mixed-conifer forest belt appears to be too dry for these giants. Actually, it is not the ancient giants with their extensive root systems that have trouble getting enough water in late summer, rather, the tiny seedlings upon which the survival of the race depends. Soil moisture studies have shown a clear correlation between water availability in the soil and sequoia distribution.

This need for water is quite possibly intensified by the fact that the seedlings require bright sunshine in which to grow, a condition that probably dries many soils beyond the point at which they can support seedling sequoias. Note carefully what this implies, for it says much about the sequoia's distribution. Not only must sequoias grow in areas of abundant soil moisture, but they also require areas with abundant sunshine. The key to this puzzle is fire. Without periodic fires, sequoias could not survive in the Sierra.

There would be enough water in the soil but not the necessary sunny spots for germination and initial growth.

The Giant Forest, with its relatively abundant annual precipitation (averaging about 45 inches [114 cm]) and its gentle slopes, collects and holds soil moisture especially well. The grove's extensive wetland meadows, almost unparalleled in the other groves, stand in clear testimony to the Giant Forest plateau's abundance of soil moisture. Here the sequoias find the moisture they need to survive and grow.

Temperature is a second apparent major factor in sequoia distribution, but not one as clearly under-stood as soil moisture. A measurable fact is that sequoias almost never establish themselves in mountain areas where extreme winter temperatures drop below zero degrees Fahrenheit (-18° C). Muir, writing in the nineteenth century, hypothesized that sequoias avoided the soils left behind by melting ice age glaciers, but that is not entirely true. What seems more likely is that sequoias have trouble establishing themselves in valleys and basins where cold winter air drains down from the high country on winter nights. Mostly, these nighttime rivers of air follow the same paths as the glaciers that once flowed from the

Fire is essential for the reproduction of the giant sequoia

Giant sequoia seedling

same mountain summits. This said, it is not clear if it is the air temperatures themselves that prevent sequoias from spreading into these areas or whether cold soil temperatures or short growing seasons prevent their success. These are some of the many things that are not known about sequoias.

The plateau of Giant Forest, located on a ridge between two deep canyons, is well protected from the winter cold that limits sequoias elsewhere. Both canyons drain cold air from the high peaks to the east safely away from the plateau's moisture-rich basins. Wolverton Creek, located just east of the grove, serves as an added protection, capturing and channeling away cold air coming down the western slopes of Alta Peak. The climatic effect can be startling. On the coldest winter nights, the heart of Giant Forest will be five to ten degrees warmer than nearby Lodgepole, barely two miles to the east of the Sherman Tree and at the same altitude. Lodgepole, which is directly down slope from the cold headwaters of the Marble Fork of the Kaweah River, has no native sequoias.

There is something more here, however. Something that is more difficult to define. Giant Forest is not just a good place for sequoias, somehow it is the best. A very high concentration of the species' biggest specimens grow in this one place. Why is that? Again, there are no definitive answers, only hypotheses.

What is known is that sequoia size is a result of several processes including growth rate and longevity. Surprisingly, the biggest trees are not always the oldest, but rather trees that have prospered and grown rapidly. Recent studies have shown the General Sherman Tree to be such a specimen. Although clearly the largest of all living sequoias, its age probably does not much exceed 2000 years and is perhaps significantly less. Since ring counts on other sequoias have sometimes exceeded 3000 years, it is apparent that longevity alone does not explain size.

The biggest sequoias, aside from being fast growing trees, usually do share a number of characteristics, however; and these may be the key to exceptional individual size. Generally, the biggest trees are single trees growing well away from other monarchs and trees that have not received particularly severe damage from fire or lightening. Critically, these biggest of the Big Trees also often share two other characteristics -- they usually grow in gentle swales with exceptionally good access to soil moisture, and they are not usually located on either very steep or nearly level terrain. This last point deserves a bit more explanation. Steep slopes challenge sequoia growth both by limiting soil moisture, which drains away faster, and by allowing hotter fires to burn, especially in the woody debris that collects around the uphill sides of the trees. Nearly level sites present an entirely different problem. Here, all too often, soils become so wet and soft in the spring that they cannot support heavy trees.

If this analysis is correct, and it is the best yet offered, then the key to the Giant Forest's concentration of very large sequoias is that it has more of the right kind of terrain than any other grove with similar acreage. What this means is that it is the gentle, rolling nature of the Giant Forest plateau itself that is the most likely key to the grove's peerless number of large sequoias. Giving weight to this hypothesis are historic descriptions of the Converse Mountain Grove of giant sequoias, the Giant Forest's nearest natural parallel. Located some twenty-five miles to the north in what is now part of the Giant Sequoia National Monument, this grove resembled the Giant Forest in both its gentle, well-watered terrain and its exceptional number of large sequoias. Unfortunately, between 1897 and 1905, loggers removed 191 million board feet of sequoia wood from Converse, a volume equal to something in excess of 300 General Sherman Trees. The destruction of Converse Basin removed from the list of old growth groves the Giant Forest's only real natural rival. Since then, the Giant Forest has stood unique in the world of sequoias.

The General Sherman is the world's largest living tree. The key to the Giant Forest's concentration of very large sequoias is that it has more of the right kind of terrain than any other grove with similar acreage

A Place for People

Giant sequoias fascinate us and always have. The human story of the Giant Forest is thus a story of reaction to wonder. It is a story of hope, science, and conscience. It is a story that is far from finished.

Nearly all the early chapters of the story are lost. Native Americans inhabited the grove at least seasonally for several thousand years, but never, it appears, in large numbers. Their signs are not hard to find-mostly in the form of bedrock mortars and midden sites-but are never extensive. The Giant Forest, it appears, was for these people a place of reoccurring, short-term habitation. It was also, undoubtedly, a place of spiritual significance, part of a larger world filled with meaning to these hunting and gathering people. Tragically, their stories of what we call the Giant Forest are lost, consumed in the great epidemics of European diseases that decimated California's native populations in the eighteenth and nineteenth centuries.

The story we can tell with confidence begins with the arrival of Euro-Americans in the middle nineteenth century. Almost from the beginning, it is a story of differing visions and conflicting values.

company of local Native American guides, brought him face-to-face with the giant sequoias for the first time. He found value in the grove, but not particularly in the trees. To Tharp, appraising the grove through the eyes of a cattle rancher, the grove's significance came not from its trees but from the summer forage available in its lush meadows. Within a few years he had taken practical possession of the grove's wetlands for cattle grazing, a use that his family would perpetuate into the early years of the twentieth century. At Log Meadow, he converted a fire-hollowed fallen sequoia into a cabin, a shelter that endures to this day.

A dozen years later, Tharp (or perhaps his hired man James Wolverton) took in a visitor at the hollow log, a thirty-seven-year-old wandering Scot named John Muir. If Tharp represented the pioneering spirit

Tharp's Log

Hale Tharp and John Muir

Hale Tharp, a 49er from Kentucky, is generally recognized as the first Euro-American to have entered the Kaweah River canyons and visited the Giant Forest. His initial visit to the grove in 1858, in the

that had extended the nation from the Appalachians to the Sierra in one short century, Muir represented something altogether different. This wanderer, traveling by himself with only a mule for company, sought not financial gain but rather knowledge and beauty.

John Muir

Muir had left his base in Yosemite Valley two months earlier with the avowed goal of learning more about the distribution and growth habits of giant sequoias. By early October, he was on Tharp's door-step. As he explored the grove, Muir came to realize that it exceeded in both extent and beauty the other groves he had visited during his journey. As he wrote later in his book *Our National Parks*, "After a general exploration of the Kaweah Basin, this part of the Sequoia belt seemed to me the finest, and I then named it 'the Giant forest'."

Burnette Haskell and George Stewart

By the late 1880s, a new generation of men with new perspectives were looking at the Giant Forest. Two with very different dreams were Burnette Haskell and George Stewart. Both projected grand dreams onto the grove's resources, dreams that history would soon bring into conflict.

Haskell first came to the Giant Forest in October 1885, exactly ten years after Muir's visit. Unlike Muir, he did not come alone, but rather in the company of a band of prospective colonists who promptly filed timber claims that encompassed the entire grove and surrounding forest lands. The dream was one of separation and independence. Haskell and his companions intended to log the Giant Forest and use its resources to establish a socialist Utopian society. They called themselves the Kaweah Colony.

George Stewart also had a dream. Like Haskell, a native of California and a son of 49er parents, Stewart found himself in the 1880s editing the Weekly Delta newspaper in Visalia, the closest significant San Joaquin Valley town to the Giant Forest. Stewart had moved to Visalia a decade earlier and had been captivated by the presence of the giant sequoias in the neighboring mountains. As Visalia and other valley towns began to grow, a local market for lumber developed, and for the first time the local forests began to have potential timber value. It didn't take Stewart long to figure out that this growing market could easily spell the doom of his treasured trees. Using his newspaper as a forum, he began a campaign to protect some of the groves for public use and enjoyment. The arrival of the Kaweah Colony and its plans to harvest trees within the Giant Forest intensified his efforts. When the colonists first filed their timber claims, Stewart asked that they be investigated before claims were granted to make sure that the land was not being taken up fraudulently by large timber companies, as was happening elsewhere in the Sierra. Eventually convinced that the colonists' claims were valid, Stewart moved forward with a campaign to create a national park a few miles to the south. In September 1890, Congress rewarded his efforts by creating Sequoia National Park, the nation's second such reserve. However, it did not include the Giant Forest.

Kaweah colonists build the Colony Mill Road to Giant Forest

10

A week later, everything changed. Without Stewart's knowledge, Congress enlarged the new park, nearly tripling its size and adding the Giant Forest plateau. The colonists, once they learned of the change, were outraged but unable to derail the turn of events that seemed to have resulted from behind-the-scenes lobbying efforts on the part of the then powerful Southern Pacific Railroad. George Stewart's dream had taken a path he had never envisioned — the Giant Forest would be preserved as a part of a national park and protected for all time.

Charles Young and Walter Fry

Once the new park was established it was prompt-ly ignored. A decade passed before any work began that would make it accessible to the public. Again, the Giant Forest attracted two men with dreams, but this time their dreams proved to be compatible.

Captain Charles Young, United State Army, arrived in the Kaweah country in May, 1903. With him were several companies of the 9th Cavalry. Young's role in the new park was to continue the protection of its resources, a task that had been assigned to the Army since 1891. His burden was that both he and his troopers were black men — "buffalo soldiers" as they were known. To this role, Young brought discipline and enormous energy, the same traits that had seen him through West Point as only the third black person to ever receive a commission there.

During the summer of 1903, Young poured his energies into the new national park and into the heretofore-neglected Giant Forest area in particular. Before the summer was over he had finished the first wagon road into the grove, extended that road to Moro Rock, fenced the General Sherman Tree to protect it, and even obtained options to buy out the private lands in the grove still held by the Tharp clan. It was a stellar performance that connected the Giant Forest to the rest of the world and made it possible for casual campers to see and enjoy the wonders of the grove.

Assisting Young that summer was a local rancher named Walter Fry. Unlike Young, however, Fry could dream of almost nothing else but sequoias. A few years earlier, while working for the lumber company that was destroying the huge trees of Converse Basin, Fry took a Sunday afternoon to count the growth rings on a tree he had just felled. By the time he finished counting 3,266 annual rings, he knew that felling the tree had been a terrible mistake. He quit logging work soon thereafter, and when civilian ranger jobs became available a decade later in the new national park, he took one. In the succeeding years, Fry not only patrolled the park's trails but also became the region's premiere naturalist. After the summer of 1913, which was the last time cavalry troops were sent to summer in Giant Forest, Fry took over as superintendent of the park and made his summer headquarters at a station he built in the heart of the Giant Forest. Although he retired from the superintendency in 1920, Fry remained a dedi-cated student of the giant sequoias until his death in 1941. In 1931, with the help of John White, he published his seminal work on sequoias — Big Trees. Through these years, Fry worked to educate the world about the secrets of the huge trees of the Giant Forest.

John White and Horace Albright

While Walter Fry worked to educate visitors about the Giant Forest, another pair of men with conflicting visions cast long shadows on the grove. One of these men was Horace Albright, Assistant Director and later Director of the National Park Service; the other was John R. White, the man Albright chose to run Sequoia National Park. The two did not often see eye to eye.

Albright brought to the Giant Forest a vision of national parks that he had worked out beginning in 1915 with Stephen Mather, the man who led the campaign to create the National Park Service and who became its founding director. Mather and Albright believed that the key to a successful national park system was broad scale public use of the parks, which they thought would lead to equally broad political support. After the end of the First World War in 1918, they applied this vision not only to places like Yosemite and Yellowstone but also to the Giant Forest, Sequoia National Park's central feature. Within a few short years, the previously limited visitor developments in Giant Forest grew almost beyond recognition. A new automobile-friendly highway to the grove opened in 1926 and provided access to newly developed campgrounds and lodges. The small tent community at Round Meadow grew to become the Giant Forest Lodge; near Beetle Rock, a cabin development called Camp Kaweah sprouted amongst the trees. Soon there were 300 campsites between Round Meadow and Sunset Rock and a commercial village complete with dance hall and motion picture theater. By the late 1920s, the sequoia grove of Giant Forest harbored a small city of the same name. This "city" had a peak summer population of several thousand!

In 1930, John White rebelled. Horrified by visitor congestion over that summer's Independence Day holiday, White wrote to Albright instructing that further development must be halted immediately and that existing development must be reduced. The Giant Forest, White asserted boldly, was being destroyed by visitor use. A seed had been planted and would bear fruit decades later.

By 1930, congestion was becoming a problem in the Giant Forest

Giant Forest Lodge, Circa 1920

Moving towards Preservation

Albright rejected White's recommendations for reducing development in the Giant Forest, but in the following decades several truths became inescapably apparent. One was that the grove's trees could not sustain endless development. The other was that something was happening to the forest — it was becoming congested with small seedling trees. It took half a century to sort out these issues.

The answer came first to the forest issue, and it came from a team of scientists. In the early 1960s, Dr. Richard Hartesveldt began his pioneering studies of the ecology of the giant sequoia. What his research team soon documented was that periodic fire was missing from the sequoia groves. In their zeal to protect the trees, the rangers of the early National Park Service had attempted to keep all fires out of the groves, including Giant Forest. The result, as John Muir could have forecast in the 1870s, was that sun loving trees, including sequoias, ceased to reproduce and that thickets of shade-tolerant firs sprouted throughout the forest. Hartesveldt's experiments with the reintroduction of fire began in an isolated sequoia grove in Kings Canyon National Park and proved to be so successful that by the late 1970s fire was brought back to the Giant Forest to take its rightful place in the workings of the forest.

The issue of over-development took longer to resolve, and in a way, Hartesvelt's scientific work helped resolve it, too. With park managers looking at giant sequoias from a more ecological perspective, the unsustainability of intense commercial development in the Giant Forest came clearly into focus. In 1980, in response to this long-overdue recognition, the Park Service committed to removing commercial facilities from the heart of Giant Forest. It took another fifteen years to implement that decision, but finally, at the end of the 1996 visitor season, the old Giant Forest Lodge was closed for good. Two years later, the last remaining commercial facilities in the grove closed. By the end of the 1999 construction season, over 280 buildings had been removed from the grove and large-scale biological restoration efforts were underway. In 2002, the heart of the grove, an area once set aside for commercial activities, reopened as an educational area.

It had taken nearly a century to bring under control the development forces let loose by Captain Young in 1903. Knowing how to love the Giant Forest without destroying it had proven far more difficult than ever anticipated.

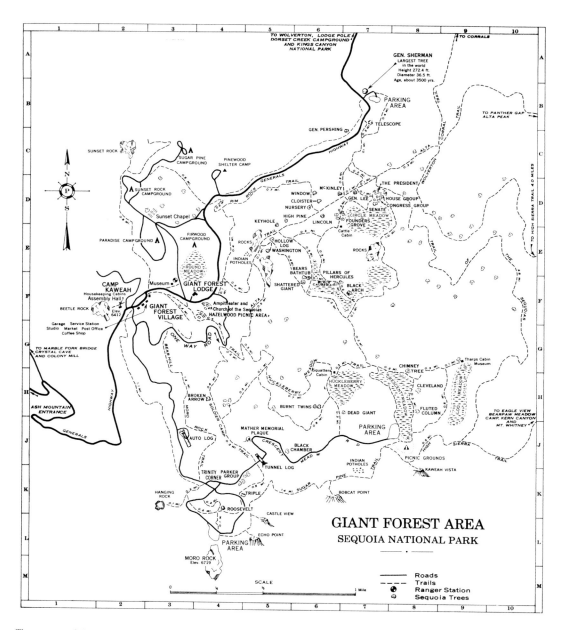

GIANT FOREST AREA
SEQUOIA NATIONAL PARK

Roads ——————
Trails – – – – –
Ranger Station
Sequoia Trees

The purpose of the national parks and the responsibility of the National Park Service are defined by Federal Law. Quoting from An Act to Establish a National Park Service, approved August 25, 1916, that purpose and responsibility are:

TO CONSERVE *the scenery and the natural historic objects and the wildlife therein, and*

TO PROVIDE FOR THE ENJOYMENT *of the same in such manner and by such means as will*

LEAVE THEM UNIMPAIRED *for the enjoyment of future generations.*

Map of Giant Forest in 1956

A Place to Explore

Seeing the Giant Forest is surprisingly easy. The place to start is the Giant Forest Museum. Located along the Generals Highway at the junction of the branch road to Moro Rock and Crescent Meadow, the museum is rich in resources to help you understand this amazing forest. Inside are exhibits that tell the story of the grove and giant sequoias.

In front of the museum is an interpretive plaza with additional exhibits and the Trail Center shelter, which is the point from which the Giant Forest's extensive trail system radiates. Walking is by far the best way to see the grove during the summer and fall, and a system of marked trails for skiing or snowshoeing makes possible the exploration of the grove during the snow season.

Opened in December 2001, the Giant Forest Museum provides a starting point to explore the world's finest grove of Giant Sequoias

Visitors wishing to explore the area will wish to purchase a detailed map of the grove. Maps can be obtained at the Giant Forest Museum as well as at other park visitor centers. Also available within the parks or by mail from the Sequoia Natural History Association (www.sequoiahistory.org) are a number of books that provide more in-depth information about the grove and Sequoia National Park.

Recommended titles:

Dilsaver, Lary and William C. Tweed: *Challenge of the Big Trees, A Resource History of Sequoia and Kings Canyon National Parks.*

Flint, Wendell: *To Find the Biggest Tree.*

Harvey, H.T., H. S. Shellhamer, R. E. Stecker, and R. C. Hartesveldt, *Giant Sequoias.*

O'Connell, Jay: *Co-Operative Dreams, A History of the Kaweah Colony.*

Strong, Douglas: *Pioneers to Preservationists, A Brief History of Sequoia and Kings Canyon National Parks.*

Tweed, William C.: *The General Sherman Tree.*

Tweed, William C.: *Kaweah Remembered, The Story of the Kaweah Colony and the Founding of Sequoia National Park.*

Willard, Dwight: *A Guide to the Sequoia Groves of California.*

"No other tree in the world . . . has looked down on so many centuries as the Sequoia, or opens such impressive and suggestive views into history."

— John Muir (1894; *Mountains of California*, 182.)

Sequoia Natural History Association

More than one million people visit Giant Forest every year. The Sequoia Natural History Association, the primary non-profit partner of the National Park Service in Sequoia and Kings Canyon National Parks enhances the visitor's experience by:

- Publishing park related books and maps.

- Operating bookstores in National Park Visitor Centers.

- Printing the free Parks' Visitor Guide.

- Conducting tours of Crystal Cave.

- Operating the Pear Lake Ski Hut.

- Running the Sequoia Field Institute.

- Managing the Beetle Rock Education Center.

- Leading educational field seminars.

- Funding park exhibits, research projects, and protection of the Parks' natural resources.

Be a part of the effort to protect places like Giant Forest through visitor education and research by joining the Sequoia Natural History Association. Members are entitled to:

- 15% off publications in Sequoia, Kings Canyon, and Devils Postpile National Monument visitor centers or by mail order.

- 10 - 20% discount on books at most other national park visitor centers.

- Discount on educational field seminars.

- Half price admission to regular Crystal Cave tours.

- Seasonal copies of the park visitor guide.

- Biannual member's newsletter.

- Invitation to the annual SNHA picnic in Sequoia.

"We are now in the mountains and they are in us, kindling enthusiasm, making every nerve quiver, filling every pore and cell of us."

— John Muir

Notes and Observations